Best of Graphis
ADVERTISING II

PAGE ONE PUBLISHING

In the case of some of the reproductions in this book it proved impossible to locate the originals, despite careful research. They were, however, considered to be of such importance that the decision was taken by the present publisher to reproduce from other published sources.

Coverphotographer : Craig Cutler

© 1993 by Graphis Press Corp., Dufourstrasse 107, CH-8008 Zürich, Switzerland

© 1993 for this edition by Page One Publishing Pte Ltd., Singapore
Distributed worldwide by Könemann Verlagsgesellschaft mbH, Bonner Str. 126, D-50968 Köln

Designed by Peter Feierabend, Berlin
Text: Peter Macho, Cologne
English translation: Michael Hulse, Cologne
French translation: Michèle Schreyer, Cologne

Printed in Singapore
ISBN 981-00-4765-7

Foreword

The sense of happiness or well-being that advertising addresses is basically a simplistic one: buy the product and your life will be a richer thing. By offering the consumer people or dreams to identify with, advertising gives him an image of himself, made glittering and magical by the product. What advertising promises is pleasure and the happy sense of being envied by others.

The promise is not usually made in as many words. The creativity departments do everything they can to put the message across in an "intelligent" way. Put bluntly, it would be an affront even to themselves. This is sensitive territory in the advertising industry, and the trade damns as stupid or aesthetically troublesome any kind of visual or linguistic stereotype, clichés, or the sorts of seriousness that border on the humourless. These were the advertising mistakes of yesteryear. Advertising now trades in humour and is ironical at its own expense. It may, for instance, include reference to itself, as in: "Ladies and gentlemen, let's get one thing straight. This poster is an invitation to go out and buy. Other people can prettify the city."

These lines from an ad for Emmental cheese are striking because they do not mention any qualities specific to the product or popularly associated with it. If the ad (which does of course picture and name the product) succeeds in provoking a positive response, it is by making us feel that Emmental advertising is up-front about its role and doesn't pretend to be doing something it's not. It is honest.

This ad, then, refers to the normal fundamental lack of credibility in advertising, in order to claim exceptional status. The idea is that we will transfer our positive response to the ad's "honesty" to the product itself. The implication is that the product is in some sense "honest" too and will fulfil its (unspoken) promise of quality.

Plainly this kind of ad has more intelligence to it than one which says soap powder X washes whiter than white. But the latter slogan may well be effective too, and perhaps the more intelligent. But whether it is clever or stupid, advertising has to work. The awkward truth is that ugly, stupid, rude and condescending ads are often as effective as smart, attractive, entertaining ones.

Fortunately, some firms that commission advertisements want high-quality ads. (Which has nothing to do with the quality of their products, as can easily be demonstrated.)

The advertising industry can be depended on to look after the quality of its own products. Throughout the world, the creative people (the adjective is theirs) have established clubs to judge advertising in their own countries and internationally. "Perhaps", one insider suspects, "they only do it to place a higher value on the art of banality and thus justify their own existence in terms other than the numerical." Be that as it may, the outcome is better quality advertising, as many of the ads in this volume, chosen from around the world, prove.

Vorwort

Die Vorstellung von Glück oder Wohlbefinden, auf die sich Werbung bezieht, ist im Grunde sehr simpel: Kaufe dieses oder jenes Produkt, und es wird dein Leben bereichern. Indem Werbung dem Konsumenten Identifikationsfiguren oder Traumszenen vorführt, bietet sie ihm ein Bild seiner selbst, das von der zu kaufenden Ware überglänzt oder verzaubert wird. Werbung verspricht Genuß und das Glück, von anderen beneidet zu werden.

Ganz direkt und ohne Umschweife wird diese Botschaft normalerweise nicht verkündet. Die Kreativen setzen alles daran, sie auf „intelligente" Weise zu vermitteln. Grob umgesetzt, erschiene sie ihnen selbst als ästhetische Zumutung. In dieser Beziehung sind die Werbeleute oft sehr empfindlich. Als „Dummheit" oder ästhetisches Ärgernis gelten vor allem sprachliche und visuelle Stereotypen, Plattitüden und ein bestimmter Ton von Ernsthaftigkeit, der an Humorlosigkeit grenzt. Das alles ist Werbung von vorgestern. Werbung von heute setzt immer häufiger auf Humor und Selbstironie. Eine Form davon ist die Produktwerbung, in der sich Werbung selbst thematisiert, zum Beispiel so: „Meine Damen und Herren, damit wir uns recht verstehen: Dieses Plakat ist eine Kaufaufforderung. Die Städte sollen andere verschönern."

Bemerkenswert an diesem Satz aus einer Werbeaktion für Emmentaler ist, daß er weder auf spezifische Eigenschaften des Produkts, für das er wirbt, noch auf irgendwelche anderen mit Emmentaler assoziierte Vorstellungen Bezug nimmt. Die positive Einstellung zu dem Produkt, das natürlich ins Bild gebracht bzw. genannt wird, erfolgt, wenn sie denn gelingt, darüber, daß der Betrachter konstatiert: Die Emmentaler-Werbung steht zu dem, was sie macht, und gibt nicht vor, etwas anderes zu sein, als sie ist. Sie ist aufrichtig.

Die sich selbst thematisierende Werbung nimmt hier Bezug auf das grundsätzliche Glaubwürdigkeitsdefizit von Werbung, um sich davon auszunehmen. Die positive Einstellung des Betrachters gegenüber ihrer „Aufrichtigkeit" soll von diesem auf das Produkt übertragen werden. Die Suggestion liegt darin, daß das Produkt selbst „ehrlich" ist und halten wird, was es, wenn auch nicht ausdrücklich, verspricht: eben ein gutes Produkt zu sein.

Ohne Zweifel ist eine solche Werbung intelligenter als die mit dem Werbespruch: „Dada wäscht so weiß, weißer geht's nicht." Wahrscheinlich wirkt aber auch dieser Spruch, und möglicherweise ist er sogar klüger als der oben genannte. Intelligent oder dumm – Werbung muß in erster Linie funktionieren. Leider ist es so, daß häßliche, dümmliche, impertinente und herablassende Werbung oft genauso zum Ziel führt wie gescheite, unterhaltsame und schöne. Zum Glück gibt es aber auch unter den Auftraggebern einige, die auf das Niveau ihrer Werbung größten Wert legen. (Das hat übrigens nichts mit der Hochwertigkeit ihrer Produkte zu tun, wie man leicht unter Beweis stellen könnte.)

Um das Niveau kümmert sich am verläßlichsten die Werbebranche selbst. In der ganzen Welt haben die „Kreativen", wie sie sich selbst gerne nennen, Clubs gegründet, deren Mitglieder jedes Jahr über die Werbung ihres Landes und auch internationaler Beiträge richten. „Vielleicht tun sie das alles nur, um der Kunst des Banalen einen höheren Sinn zu geben und damit ihrem Dasein eine andere Berechtigung als die, die sich in Zahlen ausdrücken läßt", mutmaßt ein Insider. Doch wie auch immer: Das Ergebnis solchen Strebens ist immerhin eine bessere Werbung, wovon zahlreiche der in diesem Band ausgewählten internationalen Werbebeispiele ein Zeugnis ablegen.

Préface

La publicité se réfère en fait à une très simple idée du bonheur ou du bien-être: achète ce produit-ci ou ce produit-là et ta vie en sera enrichie. En présentant au consommateur des rêves ou des personnages avec lesquels il peut s'identifier, la publicité lui offre une image de lui-même que le produit proposé va satisfaire au plus haut point ou mettre en valeur. Elle promet de la jouissance et le bonheur d'être envié.

Normalement, ce message n'est pas transmis directement. Les concepteurs font tout ce qu'ils peuvent pour le communiquer de manière intelligente. S'ils le transposaient grossièrement, ils seraient les premiers à en déplorer le manque d'esthétique. Sous ce rapport les publicistes sont souvent très sensibles. Ils considèrent avant tout comme de la «bêtise» ou une contrariété au niveau esthétique les stéréotypes linguistiques et visuels, les platitudes et un certain ton sérieux à la limite du manque d'humour. Tout cela, c'est la publicité de papa. La publicité actuelle attache de plus en plus d'importance à l'humour et l'autodérision. La publicité qui se prend elle-même pour sujet en est une forme, par exemple: «Mesdames et messieurs, comprenons-nous bien: cette affiche vous invite à acheter un produit. A d'autres d'embellir les villes.»

Ce qu'il y a de remarquable dans cette phrase tirée d'une opération publicitaire pour l'emmenthal est qu'elle ne se réfère ni à des qualités spécifiques du produit qu'elle est censée mettre en valeur, ni à d'autres idées en rapport avec le fromage en question. L'attitude positive envers le produit, qui est évidemment montré et nommé, apparaît, si la publicité atteint son objectif, lorsque l'observateur constate: la publicité pour l'emmenthal ne prétend pas être autre chose que ce qu'elle est. Elle est sincère.

Cette méthode part du fait que la publicité manque par principe de crédibilité, pour s'en excepter elle-même. Les sentiments positifs de l'observateur face à sa «bonne foi» doivent être transférés sur le produit. La suggestion est que le produit lui-même est «honnête» et va tenir, même si ce n'est pas exprimé, ce qu'il promet: c'est-à-dire être un bon produit.

Ce genre de publicité nous semble, sans aucun doute, plus intelligent que celui qui nous vante les mérites de la poudre à laver: «Dada lave plus blanc, impossible de faire mieux.» Mais cette maxime est, elle aussi, efficace et peut-être même est-elle plus avisée que celle que nous avons citée plus haut. Stupide ou intelligente, la publicité doit avant tout atteindre son objectif.

Malheureusement il arrive souvent qu'une publicité vilaine, stupide, impertinente et arrogante y arrive aussi bien qu'une publicité sensée, divertissante et belle. Par bonheur certains clients accordent une grande importance au niveau de leur publicité (ce qui, il faut le dire, n'a rien à voir avec la valeur de leurs produits, et il serait facile de le démontrer).

Le secteur publicitaire se soucie lui-même au mieux du niveau de ses réalisations. Dans le monde entier, les «créateurs», ainsi qu'ils se nomment eux-mêmes volontiers, ont fondé des clubs, dont les membres jugent chaque année la publicité de leur pays et aussi les contributions internationales. «Peut-être ne font-ils cela que pour accorder à l'art du banal une signification plus intense et donner ainsi à leur existence une autre légitimation que celle qui se laisse exprimer en chiffres», suppose un initié. Quoi qu'il en soit, la publicité y gagne et les exemples internationaux sélectionnés dans cet album en sont la preuve.

Wordt het een gewone PC of Personal System/2?

Wordt het een gewone PC of Personal System/2?

Wordt het een gewone PC of Personal System/2?

Wordt het een gewone PC of Personal System/2?

Client
IBM
Concept Directors
Ron Meijer
Henny van Varik
Machteld van der Gaag
Enrico Bartens

Art Director
Enrico Bartens (top left)
Photographer
Yves Paternoster (top right)
Illustrator
Ben Verkaaik (bottom left and right)
Photographer
Yves Paternoster

Het leven van een fiets wordt dag in dag uit belaagd.

Door regen, sneeuw, pekel, gedrang in fietsenrekken en ongemakkelijk geleun tegen ruwbeschorste bomen en muurtjes als schuurpapier.

Wil een fiets tegen die folteringen bestand zijn, dan moet hij terdege op z'n zware taak worden voorbereid.

Vandaar dat het frame van een echte Raleigh liefst 11 behandelingen ondergaat voor er één bout of meer aan wordt bevestigd.

En om aan te tonen dat dat geen woorden maar daden zijn, willen we even stapsgewijs met u doornemen wát we allemaal doen om een Raleigh onverwoestbaar te maken.

Om te beginnen wordt het frame op hoogwaardige wijze, met koper, gesoldeerd.

Dit laat echter koperresten op het frame achter, die grondig verwijderd moeten worden.

Vandaar dat de eerste behandeling bestaat uit het op electrolitische wijze in een zuurbad reinigen van het frame. (Electrolyse is het, met behulp van door vloeistof geleide electriciteit, ontbinden of vormen van chemische verbindingen).

De volgende behandeling bestaat uit het weer zuurvrij maken van het frame, waarna het in een bloedheet bad wordt uitgekookt.

Vervolgens wordt het, alweer in een electrolyse-bad, voorzien van een zinksulfaatlaag, die zowel roestwerend is als een goede hechtbasis vormt.

Na dit bad wordt de overtollige vloeistof verwijderd en wordt het frame onder hoge temperatuur gedroogd.

De zesde behandeling is cruciaal voor de levensduur van een fiets.

Daarbij wordt in een electroforese-bad, de unieke sealer dip coating aangebracht. (Bij electroforese wordt de hechting van een materiaal bevorderd door gebruik te maken van positieve en negatieve electrische ladingen).

De sealer dip coating is een unieke beschermlaag die het frame zowel van binnen als van buiten hermetisch van de buitenlucht afsluit, waardoor de kans op roestvorming praktisch nihil wordt.

Wanneer de sealer dip laag is aangebracht, gaan we over tot de afwerking van de fiets.

Het frame wordt nu licht gemoffeld, waarna het alweer op electrolitische wijze van een kleurbepalende laag wordt voorzien. Daarna wordt het weer licht gemoffeld.

De op een na laatste bewerking bestaat uit het aflakken. Dit gebeurt bij metallic frames, nog, met natte lak. Maar in alle andere gevallen wordt gebruik gemaakt van poederlak die bij voltages van 10.000 tot 40.000 op electrostatische wijze wordt aangebracht.

Het frame trekt de droge poederlak op deze wijze als een enorme magneet naar zich toe, waardoor nog geen tienduizendste millimeter wordt overgeslagen. Deze lakmethode vormt bovendien een elastische laklaag, die beter bestand is tegen beschadigingen.

Tot slot wordt het frame definitief gemoffeld, waarna het klaar is om "aangekleed" te worden. Daar waar mogelijk worden daarvoor roestvrij stalen of aluminium onderdelen gebruikt, die zowel het gewicht als de duurzaamheid van de fiets gunstig beïnvloeden. Zoals u ziet, doen we er dus alles aan om u niet alleen zo lekker, maar ook zo lang mogelijk op een Raleigh te laten fietsen.

Toch iets om in gedachten te houden wanneer u een fiets gaat kopen. Want in de winkel glimmen ze, nog, allemaal.

WAAROM WE ONZE FIETSEN ALTIJD EERST IN BAD STOPPEN VOOR WE ZE AANKLEDEN.

RALEIGH, OMDAT HET BETER FIETST ALS JE GOED ZIT.

Goed nieuws voor globetrotters. Raleigh brengt een fiets die helemaal gemaakt is voor kilometervreters.

Voor de echte avonturiers die de heuvels en kasseien beslist niet uit de weg gaan.

Zulke ritten vragen om een fiets die vederlicht en toch oersterk is. En waarop je ook bepakt en bezakt prima uit de voeten kunt.

De Raleigh Classic is zo'n fiets. Niet in de laatste plaats omdat zowel het frame als de vork gemaakt zijn van Reynolds 531 buis.

Materiaal dat z'n niet geringe faam dankt aan het feit dat het ultra licht is en toch voldoende stijfheid bezit.

Vooral dat laatste is 'n belangrijk gegeven. Want om lekker comfortabel de nodige kilometers weg te trappen is 't frame van de Classic iets langer gemaakt. Met een normale buis zou dat betekenen dat het frame gaat zwabberen.

Maar dankzij Reynolds 531 is dat bij de Classic niet het geval.

Opvallend is ook dat het leren Brooks zadel zo optimaal mogelijk boven de trappers zit. Elke pedaalslag levert daardoor het volle-rendement op.

Minstens zo belangrijk voor iemand die lange stukken fietst is de versnelling. Met deze Raleigh Classic hoef je geen heuvel uit de weg te gaan.

Want dankzij de lange arm van de achterderailleur leveren zelfs 34 tandjes geen probleem op. Tel daarbij op dat vóór niet zoals gebruikelijk twee bladen zijn gemonteerd, maar liefst drie en het is duidelijk dat je desnoods de Mont Ventoux kunt beklimmen.

Bovendien moet het een geruststellende gedachte zijn dat misschakelen praktisch uitgesloten is dankzij de klik-verstellers.

Kijken we even verder naar de bagagedragers. Die moeten natuurlijk evenals alle andere onderdelen licht en toch sterk zijn.

Kenners weten dat er maar één merk in aanmerking komt: Jim Blackburn. Die is dus zowel voor als achter gemonteerd.

Verder zijn de volgende details nog het vermelden waard. Crankstel, naven, pedalen etc. zijn allemaal van aluminium.

De wielen zijn extra versterkt. Bidonnokken zijn aangesoldeerd. En het stuur heeft Easy Rider bekleding, waardoor trillingen minder worden gevoeld.

Kortom een ideale fiets voor tochtenmakers en fietsvakantiehouders. De prijs is f 1475,-.

Hoewel niet iedere Raleigh dealer hem in voorraad zal hebben is de Raleigh Classic wel bij elke dealer te bestellen.

Voor het dichtstbijzijnde adres kunt u ook rechtstreeks bellen: T.I. Raleigh B.V., Wenckebachweg 157, 1096 AM Amsterdam, Tel.: 020 - 94 67 67.

AVONTUURLIJK TYPE ZOEKT SPORTIEVE REISGENOOT (M/V).

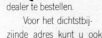

RALEIGH, OMDAT HET BETER FIETST ALS JE GOED ZIT.

Client
T. I. Raleigh
Art Director
Henny van Varik

Copywriter
Ron Meijer
Illustrator
Ben Verkaaik

7

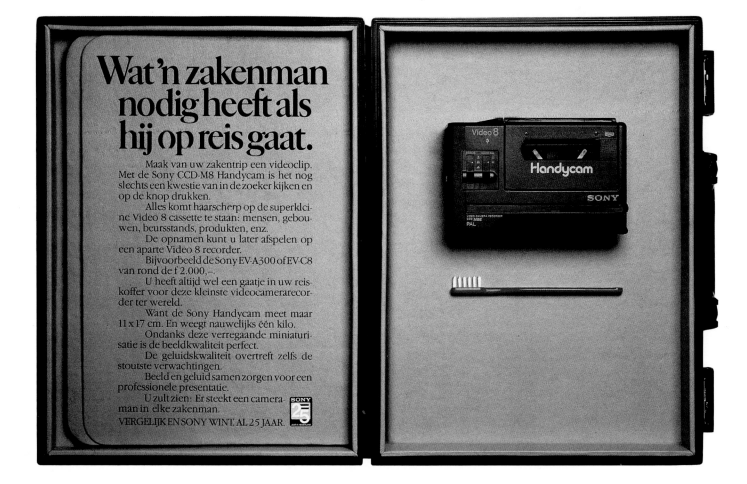

Wat'n zakenman nodig heeft als hij op reis gaat.

Maak van uw zakentrip een videoclip. Met de Sony CCD-M8 Handycam is het nog slechts een kwestie van in de zoeker kijken en op de knop drukken.

Alles komt haarscherp op de superkleine Video 8 cassette te staan: mensen, gebouwen, beursstands, produkten, enz.

De opnamen kunt u later afspelen op een aparte Video 8 recorder.

Bijvoorbeeld de Sony EV-A300 of EV-C8 van rond de f 2.000,–.

U heeft altijd wel een gaatje in uw reiskoffer voor deze kleinste videocamerarecorder ter wereld.

Want de Sony Handycam meet maar 11 x 17 cm. En weegt nauwelijks één kilo.

Ondanks deze verregaande miniaturisatie is de beeldkwaliteit perfect.

De geluidskwaliteit overtreft zelfs de stoutste verwachtingen.

Beeld en geluid samen zorgen voor een professionele presentatie.

U zult zien: Er steekt een cameraman in elke zakenman.

VERGELIJK EN SONY WINT. AL 25 JAAR.

Advertiser
Brandsteder Electronics
Art Directors
Morton Kirschner
André van Leeuwen
Copéwriter
Henk Roozendaal
Photographer
Peter Bos

Fatal Attraction.

Eigenlijk is dit een verhaal waar-aan u beter niet kunt beginnen.

Want wie eenmaal ingaat op de avances van de Sony CCD-V90E wordt onherroepelijk meegesleept in een avontuur waarvan de afloop on-voorstelbaar is.

En denk niet dat u er weerstand aan kunt bieden. Ook al meent u alles gezien te hebben.

Misschien dat het u lukt om stoï-cijns te blijven onder de fraaie bouw van deze Video 8 camcorder. Omdat u als kenner weet dat alleen schoonheid niet alles is.

Maar het is dát, wat voor het oog verborgen blijft, wat de V90 zo gevaar-lijk aantrekkelijk maakt.

Wat gaat er bijvoorbeeld door u heen als u subtiel wordt gewezen op de High Precision beeldchip, met liefst 490.000 beeldpunten, waardoor het oplossend vermogen komt op 300 lijnen. Zodat u een ongeëvenaard scherp beeld te zien krijgt.

Waar denkt u aan als u wordt geconfronteerd met de automatische witbalans en de lichtgevoeligheid voor 7 lux, waardoor deze V90 het niet laat afweten als de kaarsen aangaan?

En dat zijn nog maar een paar van de verborgen verleidingskunsten die de V90 voor u in petto heeft.

Want gaat uw fantasie niet snel-ler werken, als u weet dat de Auto-Iris altijd een juiste lichtsterkte-instelling biedt?

En dat u voor werkelijk speciale effecten de diafragma-opening ook

met de hand kunt bespelen? Dit laat-ste kunt u overigens ook doen met de Auto-Focus.

De V90 is geen alledaags type, in-derdaad. Maar wij vermoeden dat er bij menigeen een waarschuwings-lampje gaat branden, wanneer wij het volgende karaktertrekje ontsluieren.

Deze Video 8 camcorder is na-melijk een van de weinige die u met een elektronische sluiter verwennen.

Waardoor u nu volop in snelheid kunt variëren van 1/50, 1/120, 1/500, 1/1000 en, schrik niet, 1/2000.

Dit komt neer op zo'n 40 beeld-jes per seconde en verraadt meteen

de professionele trekjes van dit type.

Dit laatste wordt overigens onderstreept door de 6x Motorzoom, die traploos werkt.

En wie graag een beetje tegen-spel biedt, zorgt ervoor dat hij altijd de Macrolens achter de hand heeft. Waardoor het onderwerp tot op enke-le centimeters benaderd kan worden.

Maar er is nog meer dat de V90 zo begeerlijk maakt.

Zoals het verrukkelijk extrava-gante Data Display System, dat tot het jaar 2015 de datum en de tijd van uw opnamen bijhoudt.

Of het Lineaire Bandteller Dis-

play, dat aangeeft of er op een gebruik-te cassette nog speelduur resteert en hoeveel precies.

En nog is deze bron van plezier niet opgedroogd. Want hebt u al eens het genoegen van Edit Search mogen smaken?

De techniek die de vele hande-lingen tussen opnemen en weergeven overbodig maakt.

En u direct de juiste plek op de band te zien geeft, terwijl de camera gewoon in de opnamestand blijft.

U kunt dus meteen doorgaan met opnemen. Een naadloze overgang is mogelijk dank zij de roterende wiskop.

Overigens moet u beslist weten dat deze Video 8 geen taboes kent.

Wat u opneemt wordt storing-vrij weergegeven in slow-motion of zelfs stilstaand. Stoorstrepen worden effectief voorkomen door toepassing van een dubbele kop.

Verder heeft de V90 nòg een eigenschap waarvoor u beslist niet on-gevoelig zult zijn.

U weet bij dit type namelijk direct en op een ondubbelzinnige manier waaraan u toe bent, omdat u meteen kunt terugzien wat u opgenomen hebt.

In zwart/wit, op de ingebouwde zoeker en in kleur op elke kleuren-tv,

dank zij de bijgeleverde antennekabel.

Dat u zich gerust met de V90 kunt laten zien mag inmiddels duidelijk zijn.

Zoals het net zo prettig is om te weten dat u direct kunt overspoelen naar iedere andere videorecorder, dank zij de directe audio- en video-aansluiting.

Tja, en de kenners onder u weten al genoeg als we, misschien ten overvloede, wijzen op de onberispe-lijke FM geluidsweergavetechniek.

Waar men in Sony kringen overi-gens wel patent op lijkt te hebben.

Het zou ons niet verbazen indien u nu meteen aanstalten maakt om de V90E te ontmoeten.

Maar wij mogen u eerlijkheids-halve niet verzwijgen wat het fatale element in deze attractie kan zijn. De Sony CCD-V90E ligt helaas niet zomaar binnen ieders bereik. Ook al wilt u betalen met The Card van Sony.

Om dit type te kunnen veroveren, kunt u het best intekenen bij de Sony dealer. Vervolgens zult u dan enig geduld (en f 4995,-) moeten opbrengen voordat uw fantasie een feit wordt.

Maar dat is de beproeving van het wachten meer dan waard.

Sony Nederland B.V., Jan van Gentstraat 119, 1171 GK Badhoevedorp.

Vergelijk.... en Sony Video 8 wint.

SONY

NAPIER IS NAPIER.

NAPIER IS SHAPELIER.

NAPIER IS SHOWIER.

$12.50. Bracelet, $15.

Clip-on pierced earrings, $9 and $10.

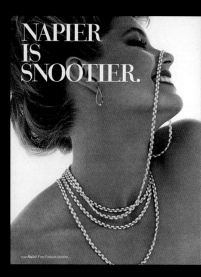

NAPIER IS SNOOTIER.

Copywriter
Anne Conlon
Photographer
Bill Helburn

In 1502, this mark was created by master printer Aldus Manutius of Venice. It expressed his lifelong devotion to the principles of originality, artistry, and superb craftsmanship. A similar dedication to those high standards is reflected in today's IBM* typewriters. With the IBM "Executive"* Typewriter, your correspondence is enriched by the look of fine printing...to create impressions beyond words.

Lucantonio Giunta of Florence created this mark for his press in 1563. An artist as well as a master printer, he spared no effort to make it a symbol of originality, distinction, and devoted craftsmanship. A similar dedication produces today's IBM* typewriters. That is why the IBM "Executive"* Typewriter can add the unique quality of fine printing to your correspondence...create impressions beyond words.

Client
IBM
Additional creatives
Bob Larimer

11

Advertiser
Ognibeni & Co.
Art Directors
André van Leeuwen
Morton Kirschner

Copywriter
Wim Michels
Photographers
Martin Woods
Michael Steenmeijer

Ihr Hausarzt sagt, Sie sind fällig. Ihr Finanzamt sagt, Sie sind dran. Wo liegt das Problem, denken Sie, buchen Condor und tauchen erst mal unter.

⊗ Condor
Die Ferienflieger der Lufthansa

Mädchen sind langweilig und doof, sagte Ihr Sohn noch zu Hause. Dann steigen Sie mit ihm aus der Condor, und plötzlich ist er nur noch mit seiner kleinen Señorita unterwegs.

⊗ Condor
Die Ferienflieger der Lufthansa

Sie haben's zu was gebracht: zu Termindruck, Auftragsjagd und Erfolg. Und dann guckt Sie Ihr Hund plötzlich voller Mitleid an, und Sie gehen ins Reisebüro und fragen, wohin die Condor fliegt.

⊗ Condor
Die Ferienflieger der Lufthansa

3 Mathearbeiten, 4 Diktate, 2 verschrammte Knie und 1 Schnupfen. Dann steigen Sie mit dem kleinen Kerl aus der Condor, und plötzlich ist alles vergessen.

⊗ Condor
Die Ferienflieger der Lufthansa

Ihr Chef meint, Sie sollten mehr arbeiten. Ihr Freund meint, Sie sollten weniger arbeiten. Ihre Mutter meint, Sie sähen so blaß aus. Wir meinen, Sie haben längst einen Urlaub mit Condor verdient.

⊗ Condor
Die Ferienflieger der Lufthansa

Die Wohnung, die Sie mit Ihrer Freundin teilen, ist Ihnen zu eng. Das Großraumbüro geht Ihnen auf den Nerv. Sie fliegen mit Condor. Und plötzlich macht es Ihnen überhaupt nichts aus, Ihr schmales Handtuch zu teilen.

⊗ Condor
Die Ferienflieger der Lufthansa

Client
Condor Flugdienst GmbH
Art Director
Wolfgang Leihener
Creative Director
Klaus Erich Küster
Photographer
Michael Ehrhart
Agency
Michael Conrad & Leo Burnett GmbH & Co. KG

EIN SLIP
SOLL SICH DER
ANATOMIE DES
MANNES ANPASSEN.
UND NICHT
UMGEKEHRT.

WENN EINE EINHORN-BLUSE EIN EINHORN-HEMD TRIFFT

RETTE SICH,
WER KANN...
IN DIESEN
HAUSMANTEL
VON JOCKEY.

SOLCH EIN PYJAMA
IST EIN
SCHLAFMITTEL
MIT TRAUMHAFTEN
NEBENWIRKUNGEN.

Client
Jockey Volma
Wirkwaren GmbH
Art Director
Uli Weber
Creative Directors
Brigitte Fussnegger
Uli Weber
Designer
Ursel Koch
Photographer
Klaus Hagmeier
Agency
Leonhardt & Kern
Werbung GmbH

EIN URLAUB
OHNE BADE-SHORTS
IST WIE EIN
STRAND OHNE MEER.

JOCKEY

STREICHELEINHEIT
MIT
ZWEI ÄRMELN.

JOCKEY

JETZT TRÄGT MAN
ROSEN
UNTER DEN HOSEN.

JOCKEY

WEIL
MAN NIE WEISS,
WIE DER TAG
ENDET.

JOCKEY

Client
Jockey
Art Director
Uli Weber
Creative Directors
Brigitte Fussnegger
Uli Weber
Copywriters
Brigitte Fussnegger
Uli Weber
Photographer
Klaus Hagmeier
Agency
Leonhardt & Kern
Werbung GmbH

EVERY YEAR, THOUSANDS OF PEOPLE GO TO THE ONE SHOW AWARDS DINNER.

BUT ONLY 79 ENJOY THEIR MEALS.

THE ONE CLUB FOR ART & COPY INC. 3 WEST 18TH STREET, NEW YORK, NY 10011 / 212-255-7070

Art Director
Peter Cohen
Copywriter
Larry Spector

Art Directors
Clement Mok
Hugh Dubberly
Creative Directors
Thom Marchonna
Hugh Dubberly
Designers
Steve Seiler
Tim Brennan
Copywriters
Linda Bradford
Thom Marchonna
Production Artists
Jan Marti
Patty Taylor
Production coordinator
Heather Furmidge
Photographers
Paul Matsuda
Various Stock
Illustrator
Michael Schwab

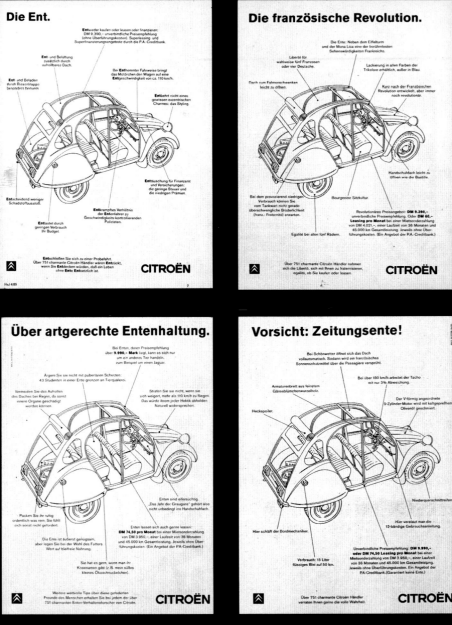

Die Ent.

Die französische Revolution.

Über artgerechte Entenhaltung.

Vorsicht: Zeitungsente!

CITROËN

Client
Citroën Automobil AG
Art Director
Andrea Wark
Creative Director
Werner Butter
Designer
Martin Teschner
Illustrator
Herbert-Clemens Toups

Für Ihren

nächsten

Citroën

haben wir

den

übernächsten

gebaut.

CITROËN

Citroën

hat

etwas

Besseres

als

Federn.

CITROËN

Citroën

bietet

die

preiswerteste

Möglichkeit,

nach

Australien

zu kommen.

CITROËN

CITROËN

Client
Citroën Automobil AG
Art Director
Andrea Wark
Designer
Martin Teschner
Agency
RSCG, Butter, Rang GmbH

THREE OF THE MOST SOPHISTICATED POWER PLANTS IN THE WORLD AREN'T NUCLEAR.

Truly advanced technology is not the sole province of assorted power plants that energize great cities. It is also evident in certain mobile power plants that propel people from one of those cities to the next. And to every point in between.

Residing under the hood of the BMW 528e, for example, is an inspired paradox—the Eta power plant. Where the traditional engine accepts a loss of response as a fair price to pay for fuel efficiency, the Eta engine actually develops higher torque (power) at engine speeds at which a car is most often driven. At the same time achieving an efficiency (EPA-estimated 20 mpg, 25 mpg highway*) once thought impossible in a performance sedan. In effect, defying that enemy of innovation known as convention.

The 524td turbo diesel has vastly accelerated the cause of diesels in their evolution from mere contraption to true BMW.

In fact, the BMW 524td turbo diesel is the quickest diesel ever to grace our roads.

And the 535i contains an in-line six-cylinder power plant that is actually fueled by information as well as gasoline. It's equipped with a microprocessor-based engine management system that gathers information from sensors. It utilizes this data to calculate the exact amount of fuel to inject into each cylinder at the precise moment for optimum ignition. The result is a veritable "land rocket" (Car and Driver) with a pulse-stirring 0-60 acceleration of 7.4 seconds that makes it the fastest BMW in America.

In sum, the 5-Series BMW's not only convert fuel into energy, but also manage to convert energy into electrifying fun.

If you'd like a firsthand demonstration of this phenomenon, visit one of your BMW dealers soon.

THE ULTIMATE DRIVING MACHINE.

*Figures are for comparison purposes only. Your actual mileage may vary depending on speed, weather and trip length. Actual highway mileage will most likely be lower.
© 1985 BMW of North America, Inc. The BMW trademark and logo are registered.

BMW 528e
BMW 524td
BMW 535i

Client
BMW
Art Director
Jerry Whitley
Copywriter
Larry Spector
Photographer
Jeffrey Zwart
Agency
Ammirati & Puris

Why Should The Rich Get All The Brakes?

How much money you have in your bank account shouldn't determine how safe you feel on the road.

And if you purchase the new 1990 Subaru® Legacy,™ it won't.

The Subaru Legacy is one of the few affordable cars in the world with anti-lock brakes (ABS). A feature that pumps your brakes for maximum maneuverability under heavy braking.

It's a safety feature so valuable, some insurance companies will give you a refund on your premium if you buy a car with the ABS system.

Even without anti-lock brakes, the Subaru Legacy offers you one of the most advanced systems for controlling your car on the road today. With full time four wheel drive — a more civilized form of four wheel drive that gives you better handling and traction on four lane highways as well as one lane dirt roads. Power-assisted front and rear disc brakes. And four wheel independent suspension.

Of course, to many drivers, how fast they go is just as important as how fast they stop. So every Subaru Legacy is powered by a horizontally-opposed (for reduced vibration), aluminum (for more even heat distribution), single overhead camshaft, multi-point electronic fuel injected, 16 valve engine.

The Subaru Legacy was also designed to stand up to the very same conditions that have driven many cars into the ground.

In fact, 93% of all Subaru cars registered in America since 1979 are still on the road.* And a new Subaru may last even longer. A Subaru Legacy has broken the FIA world speed/endurance record by running 19 days at an average speed of 138.8 mph for more than 60,000 miles.**

Since the Subaru Legacy was designed to last a long time, it's available with a lot of things to make that time pass pleasantly. Including power sunroof, power windows and locks, lumbar support seats and an 80 watt AM/FM stereo radio.

And you get all of this for thousands of dollars less than the cost of many European luxury cars.

But the way we figure, along with the anti-lock brakes, you deserve a few other breaks as well.

*R.L. Polk & Co. Statistics, July 1, 1988. **Validated by the Fédération Internationale De L'Automobile. †Suggested retail price. Does not include dealer preparation, inland transportation costs, license and state or title fees. Dealer's actual price may vary. ‡Based on manufacturer's suggested retail price.

Mercedes 190E with ABS Brakes, $31,600.†

Jaguar XJ6 with ABS Brakes, $39,700.†

BMW 535i with ABS Brakes, $42,310.†

Subaru Legacy™
We Built Our Reputation By Building A Better Car.

1990 Subaru Legacy with Full Time Four-Wheel Drive and ABS Brakes, from $18,914.

TO ENJOY SIGNIFICANT SAVINGS ON THIS HIGH-PERFORMANCE IMPORT, EXPORT YOURSELF.

Let BMW underwrite your next trip to Europe.

You'll save up to 12% by acquiring your BMW in Europe. Which may pay for the entire trip itself.

And you'll be taking in Europe's scenery while traveling in accommodations immeasurably more pleasurable, yet vastly less expensive than the average rent-a-car.

And we do all the work. So your mind doesn't labor while the rest of you is on vacation.

THE 1985 BMW EUROPEAN DELIVERY PROGRAM.

Does your food keep you up at night?

To stop the noise in our neighborhood
you've got to make some.
Call Project Quiet City (212) 362-4942

Sponsored by Citizens for a Quieter City, Inc., The American Red Cross Building, 150 Amsterdam Ave., New York, N.Y. 10023

Almost every electric appliance was invented to save time. Salton Hotray was invented to stop time.

Like most things in life, cooking and enjoying food is a matter of timing. It takes a lot of time to prepare fine foods correctly. But, it takes very little time to ruin them. If you could stop time at exactly the moment your foods were done, you'd stop them from becoming cold or overcooked and dried out.

That's precisely what Salton Hotray electric food keeper does.

Its radiant heat surface is thermostatically controlled to keep food just under the cooking point. So when you place your carefully prepared foods on Salton Hotray electric food keeper, it keeps them hot, juicy, and flavorful.

That significant fact may make Salton Hotray the most versatile kitchen appliance.

For example, with Salton Hotray, the meat will wait for the potatoes, the potatoes will wait for the sauce, the sauce will wait for the vegetables. As each food is ready, put it on Salton Hotray, where it will stay hot and fresh and juicy.

And if someone is working late, or guests arrive late, or someone wakes up late, their food will taste as though they'd been right on time.

You can serve directly from Salton Hotray, right in the dining room, to have second helpings that taste identical to firsts.

Salton Hotray is not an appliance you'll use for a few weeks, then put on a shelf. It can help all the time, at every hot meal of the year.

Considering all the benefits of the Salton Hotray electric food keeper, there's something even more amazing than its ability to stop time, and that's all the time you've done without it.

Salton Hotray is available in many models from about $19* to $175*.

For a complete catalogue of Salton products, write Salton Inc., 1260-C Zerega Avenue, Bronx, New York 10462.

*Manufacturers suggested retail prices. Underwriters Laboratories Listed.

Salton Hotray

Client
Friends of the animals
Art Director
Sal de Vito
Copywriter
Larry Spector
Photographer
Cailor Resnick

Client
Perrier-Jouet
Art Director
Ron Brello
Copywriter
Larry Spector
Agency
Levine, Huntley,
Schmidt & Beaver

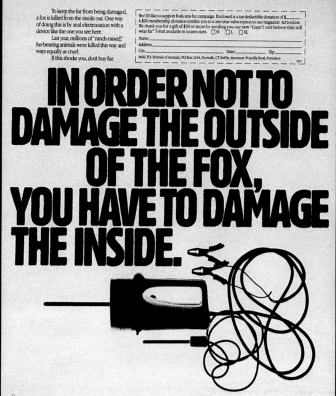

To keep the fur from being damaged, a fox is killed from the inside out. One way of doing this is by anal electrocution with a device like the one you see here.

Last year, millions of "ranch-raised," fur-bearing animals were killed this way and ways equally as cruel.

If this shocks you, don't buy fur.

IN ORDER NOT TO DAMAGE THE OUTSIDE OF THE FOX, YOU HAVE TO DAMAGE THE INSIDE.

Friends of Animals

If It's Difficult For People To Get Into The Social Register, Imagine How Hard It Is For A Grape.

SINCE 1887, THE SOCIAL REGISTER HAS DEEMED ONE CHAMPAGNE TO BE SOCIALLY ACCEPTABLE.

CHAMPAGNE
PERRIER-JOUËT
EPERNAY-FRANCE

Imported by Seagram Chateau & Estate Wines Co., New York, N.Y.

Client
Citizens for a quieter New York
Art Director
Bill Weinstein
Copywriter
Larry Spector
Photographer
Alan Dolgins
Agency

Client
Salton Inc.
Art Director
Ron Brello
Copywriter
Larry Spector
Photographer
Michael O'Neill
Agency

アタマがしわくちゃ。

Advertiser
Cosmo Securities Co., Ltd.
Art Director
Tsuguya Inoue
Creative Directors
Humichika Kato
Taisuke Okano
Designers
Tsuguya Inoue
Seiai Hirota
Copywriter
Hiroyuki Yoshimukra
Stylist
Masako Koiso
Photographer
Minsei Tominaga

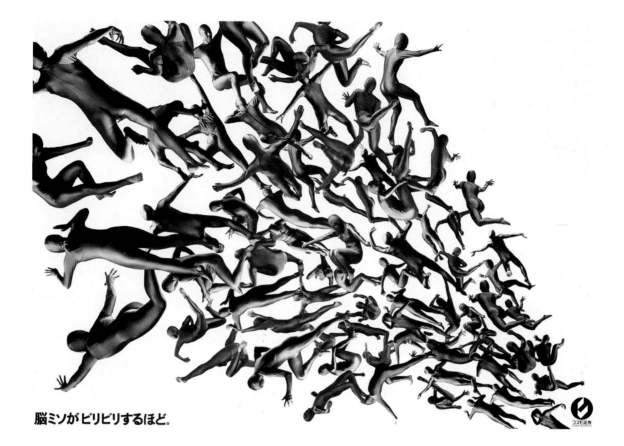

脳ミソがビリビリするほど。

Art Director
Hiroshi Yonemura
Creative Director
Masaaki Izumiya
Copy Director
Junkichi Uemura
Designers
En Chiba
Cazuma Yoshikawa
Advertiser
Tokyo Metropolitan
Racing Association
Copywriters
Kazuya Koshimo
Tomoshi Saida
Photographer
Bin - Shun

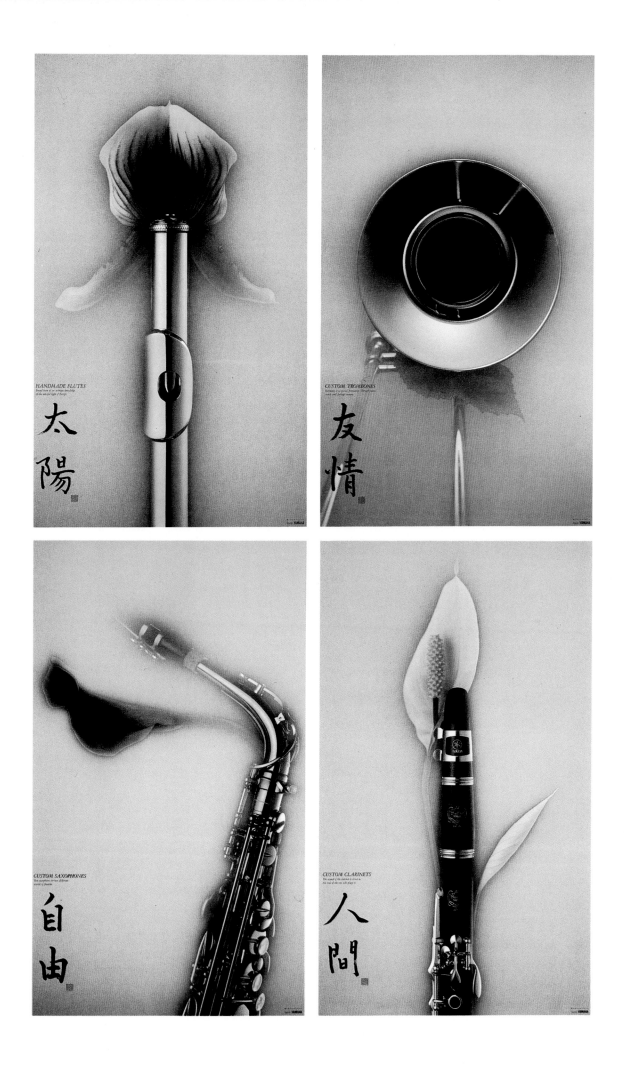

HANDMADE FLUTES
太陽

CUSTOM TROMBONES
友情

CUSTOM SAXOPHONES
自由

CUSTOM CLARINETS
人間

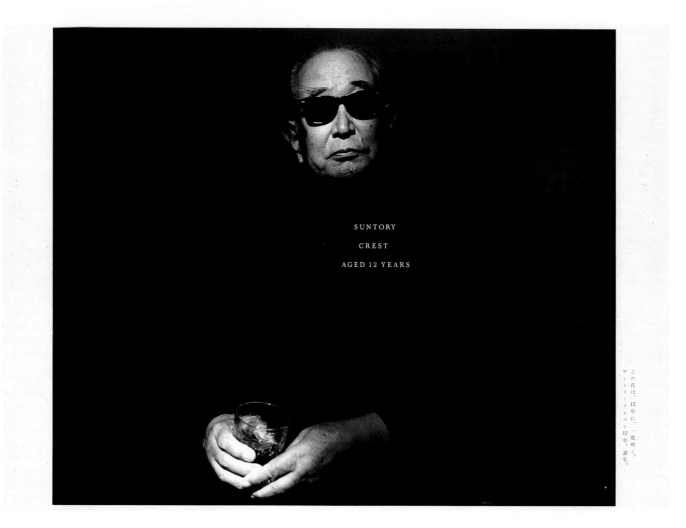

SUNTORY

CREST

AGED 12 YEARS

この花は、12年に、一度咲く。サントリークレスト12年。誕生。

Advertiser
Suntory Ltd.
Art Director / Designer
Yoshihiro Kobayashi
Copywriter
Noboru Kimura
Photographer
Yoshihiko Ueda

BLOUSON/WF-J11-020/¥18,000/ ●RED ●MOCHA ●DARK BROWN ●BLACK

THIS COLOR IS BLACK, RED

PEA COAT/WF-J09-129/¥32,000/ ●MOCHA ●DARK BROWN ●BLACK

THIS COLOR IS MOCHA

Advertiser
Y's For Men Inc.
Art Director / Designer
Yasuhiro Sawada
Photographer
Kazuyasu Hagane

Client
Nike
Typography / Design
Michael Prieve, George Vogt
Agency
Wieden & Kennedy

Client
Nike
Typography / Design
Michael Prieve
Pittman Hensley
Agency
Wieden & Kennedy

Client
Nike
Typography / Design
Michael Prieve
Agency
Wieden & Kennedy

Client
Nike
Typography/Design
Michael Prieve
Agency
Wieden & Kennedy

Client
Zanders Feinpapiere AG
Typography/Design
Ton van Bragt
Héléne Bergmans
Marc van Bokhoven
Studio
Studio Dumbar

"I heard dinner. I never heard diner."

REAL LIVE LEGS
Liz claiborne

"I swear my next apartment will have an elevator."

REAL LIVE LEGS
Liz claiborne

Art Director
Steven Mitsch
Copywriter
Rosalind Greene
Agency
Altschiller Reitzfeld
Tracy Locke

"I knew they weren't expecting a crowd, but this is ridiculous."

REAL LIVE LEGS
Liz claiborne

"Now if I could only find a jug of wine and thou."

REAL LIVE LEGS
Liz claiborne

Client
Daichi Co., Ltd.

Masayuki Kurokawa

*The traditional Japanese technique of applying
color to copper has been called upon in the creation
of this copper-alloy tableware series.*

Manufacturer: Takenaka Works Co., Ltd.
Logotype & Poster Design: Shin Matsunaga. Photo: Noritsyo Nakamoto

Client:
Daichi Co., Ltd.

Client
Office of the Mayor
of New York
Art Director
Peter Cohen
Creative Director
Michael Smith
Copywriter
Peter Cohen
Photographer
Stock
Agency
Chiat / Day / Mojo

Client
Minnesota Department
of Health
Art Director
Wendy Hansen
*Creative Director /
Copywriter*
Lyle Wedemeyer
Photographer
Rick Dublin
Agency
Martin / Williams

Client
Clean Land
Art Director
Bill Schwartz
Creative Director
Chris Perry
Copywriter
Joyce Spetrino
Illustrator
David Fitch
Agency
Meldrum and Fewsmith

Client
Save the world
Art Director
Cabell Harris
Copywriter
Mike Lescarbeau
Illustrator
Various
Photographer
Jack Richmond

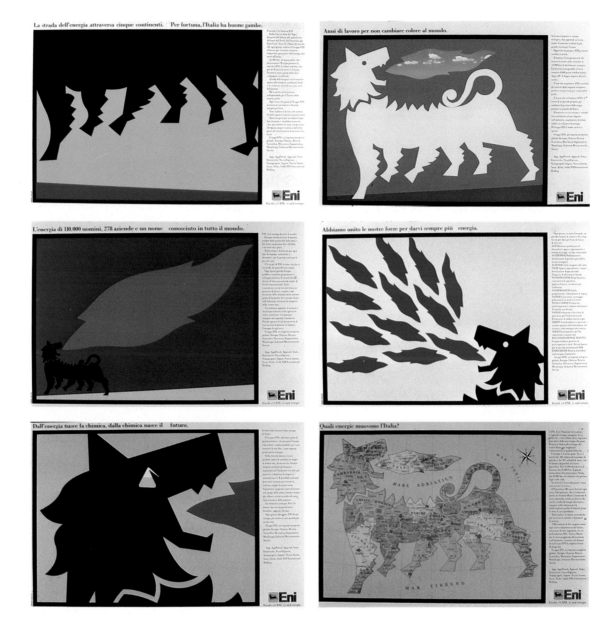

Trade and Corporate
Press Campaign for ENI
Creative Directors
Maurizio Sala
Lorenzo Marini

Photographer
Günther Raupp

A three-year old boy saluting
at his father's funeral.

A woman crying over
the body of a student shot
by the National Guard.

An American President lifting his
pet beagle up by its ears.

A lone student standing
in front of four tanks.

© 1990 Nikon Inc.

If you can picture it in your head, it was probably taken with a Nikon.

Nikon
We take the world's greatest pictures®

Client
Nikon
Art Director
Ron Rosen
Creative Directors
Larry Cadman
Earl Cavanah
Copywriter
Richard Kelley
Agency
Scali, McCabe, Sloves

AS BROUGHT TOGETHER by the Scanmaster Scanner/AM Mask Gun. © FOR COLOR INC. Color separation and FujiFilm Exposure. 498 E. 9th St., Milwaukee, WI 53204. 414.291.4950. Toll free 1.800.377.7303.

Charles & Di

Client
For Color Inc.
Art Directors
Mike Wheaton
Todd Treleven
Creative Director
Tom Jordan
Copywriter
Mike Wheaton
Agency
Hoffman York & Compton

After years of buying everything from the "Porsche of toasters" to the "Porsche of stereos," perhaps you're ready for the Porsche of cars.

There is a small group of individuals in the world for whom perfection is almost an obsession. Somewhere in the evolution of this group's vernacular, the name Porsche came to represent far more than sheetmetal. It became a benchmark.

For their part, these purists have used Porsche as an analogy for anything inimitable. For our part, we have continued to craft unique, exciting automobiles which make the analogy viable.

The new 944 S2 Cabriolet is a powerful basis for such comparison.

The 944 convertible continues a tradition of racebred, open-top cars. Professor Porsche's first car, an open roadster hand-built in 1948, won the first race it entered. Thus began the story.

The 944 chapter opened in 1981, when the car was created for the famous 24 hour race at LeMans. The new Cabriolet possesses the engineering that has since made the 944 victorious on racetracks around the globe.

A transaxle design provides near-perfect 50-50 weight balance. Cornering is uncannily stable. Pressure-cast alloy wheels are mated to huge, 4-piston internally vented disc brakes with ABS. Suspension, steering, braking and drive systems are all carefully matched to work as one. Even tire tread is meticulously calculated. (Obsessive enough for you?)

The painting process alone requires 26 steps. Body parts are hot-dip zinc galvanized before a single weld is done, sealing zinc even in the seams to prevent corrosion. (To weld through these panels, we had to develop our own tools.)

So after nearly a decade of setting standards against which other sports cars are measured, about the only way left to make the 944 more fun was to take the top off. Naturally, in typical Porsche fashion.

The thick, 4-layer top is hand-stitched, then hand-assembled. For a precise fit on each individual car. The Porsche philosophy is that a convertible must truly be 4-season. A specially reinforced windshield sweeps air around the vehicle, creating an effect that has been described as "like being in the eye of a hurricane." An eerie calm, with a tempest swirling about you.

For those who measure value strictly in terms of exclusivity, we offer this thought; just over 1,600 of these 1990 Cabriolets will be made available in the U.S. Or, to put it another way, fewer than 140 per month for the entire country.

If you have spent a lifetime acquiring a collection of preeminent products, and are now ready for the automobile which inspired many of them, we invite you to visit your authorized Porsche dealership for a test-drive.

As a final side-benefit, you can also experience our new 4x25 watt Reno II sound system. It is, in fact, the Porsche of stereos.

The new Porsche 944 S2 Cabriolet.

Everything you really need to know about the Turbo Z.

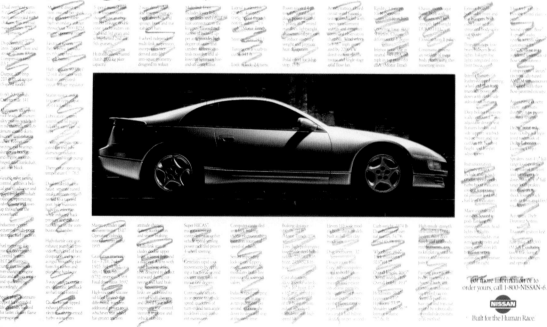

For more information or to order yours, call 1-800-NISSAN-6.

NISSAN

Built for the Human Race.

Client	*Client*
Porsche Cars	Nissan Motor
North America	Corporation
Art Director	*Art Directors*
Mark Johnson	Corey Stolberg
Creative Director	Chuck Bennett
Pat Burnham	*Creative Director*
Copywriter	Lee Clow
John Stingley	*Copywriter*
Photographer	Tom Witt
Jeff Zwart	*Photographer*
Agency	Bob Grigg
Fallon McElligott	*Agency*
	Chiat / Day / Mojo

WE DON'T SERVE LUNCH.

IT TAKES US ALL DAY TO PREPARE DINNER.

RESTAURANT · BUTLER SQUARE · MINNEAPOLIS

Client
D'Amico Cucina
Art Director
Bob Brihn
Creative Director
Pat Burnham
Copywriter
Bruce Bildsten
Agency
Fallon McElligott

The best place to eat next to Positano.

The Art Directors Club. Where our $9.95 all-you-can-eat buffet lunch buys you everything from superb salads and simmering stews to pasta, omelettes and burgers.

There's plenty of interesting side dishes, too: Lectures on the delicacies of typography. Discussions on the ingredients of good design. And exhibits that will satisfy your hunger for great work.

Call 674-0500 and see what's cooking at the Art Directors Club. Considering everything we serve, you could say Positano is the best place to eat next to us.

The Gallery Restaurant at the Art Directors Club
250 Park Avenue South, NY, NY 10003 212-674-0500

CREATED BY CALET, HIRSCH & SPECTOR, INC.   TYPE COURTESY VISUAL ARTS PRESS LTD.

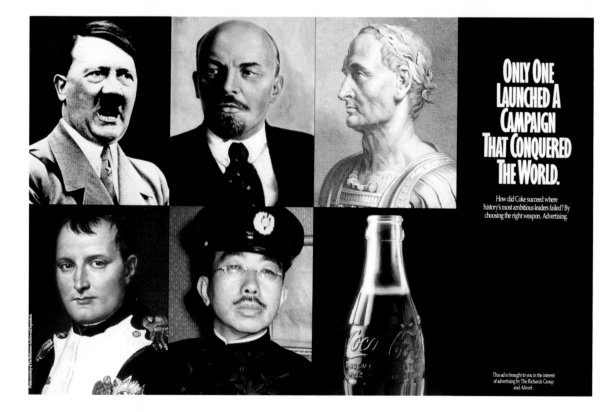

ONLY ONE LAUNCHED A CAMPAIGN THAT CONQUERED THE WORLD.

How did Coke succeed where history's most ambitious leaders failed? By choosing the right weapon. Advertising.

This ad is brought to you in the interest of advertising by The Richards Group and Adweek.

Client	Client / Agency
The Art Directors Club	The Richards Group
Art Directors	*Art Directors*
Anna Suplina	Tom Gilmore
Gordon Bennett	Christopher Gyorgy
Creative Director	*Creative Director*
Peter Hirsch	Stan Richards
Copywriters	*Designer*
Steven Landsberg	Christopher Gyorgy
Hal Katkov	*Copywriters*
Agency	James Boyce
Calet, Hirsch & Spector	Mike Renfro
	Photographer
	John Wong

WAT DENKT U, ZOU HET BIJ
ONS WEL LOSLOPEN MET AIDS?

De Wereld Gezondheidsorganisatie heeft 1 december uitgeroepen tot Wereld AIDS Dag.

Vandaag denkt de wereld na over AIDS. In sommige landen hebben ze daar geen speciale dag voor nodig. In delen van Noord-Amerika, Afrika en het Caraïbisch gebied worden mensen al dagelijks met de ziekte geconfronteerd.

In ons land gaat het tot vandaag de dag om plusminus duizend mensen met AIDS en enkele tienduizenden mensen die met het virus besmet zijn. Dat lijkt allemaal mee te vallen. Toch mogen we niet vergeten dat de situatie rond AIDS allesbehalve rooskleurig is.

Vandaar dat we gerichte hulp blijven verlenen en blijven voorlichten. Vandaar activiteiten zoals de AIDS-infolijn (06-0 22 22 20; gratis) en het AIDS Fonds (giro 8957).

En vandaar allerlei activiteiten in internationaal verband.

Tientallen organisaties spannen zich dagelijks in. Van GGD tot junkiebond, van jongerenorganisatie tot vakbond, van COC tot NOS, van buddy tot verpleger.

Maar als u werkelijk wilt dat het bij ons in Nederland niet zo'n vaart zal lopen, zullen we er zelf heel veel aan moeten doen. En er soms iets voor moeten laten. Niet alleen vandaag. **DENK NA. STOP AIDS.**

Client
NCAB Projectgroep
Voorlichting
Art Director
Rob van Vijfeyken

Creative Directors
Harry Obdejin
Bart Hammer
Copywriter
André Dammers

Photographer
Hans Kroeskamp
Illustrator
Silvan Steenbrink
Agency
PMSVW / Y & R

One of our writers on China knows so much, we can't begin to tell you about him.

In June 1989, he was a student protesting in Tiananmen Square. He avoided the tanks. He avoided arrest. Now, incredibly, he's a Chinese ministry official, pushing democracy from the inside.

When we wanted an article on China one year after the student uprising, he was perfect to write it. Who is he? We can't tell you. That was part of the deal.

At World Monitor magazine, we believe highly involved stories call for highly involved writers. Experts who have been there. Who possess unique knowledge, and understand its significance.

We go wherever we have to in the world to find them. From Communist officials, to American schoolteachers, to former presidents. Then, we let them explain things in their own words. For an insider's perspective no journalist could uncover in a traditional interview.

It's the kind of insight needed to understand complex global issues. That's why the people you find reading World Monitor, like the people who write for it, are leaders. Individuals looking for informed assessments and speculation on what may come next, so they can prosper in the global village-we all now share.

World Monitor. Conceived, created and followed by those who understand that in today's world there is, more than ever, no substitute for experience.

Where the people in the news report the news.

For 100 Years Our Students Have Been Known For Their Imagination.

Artists have always possessed the special gift of redefining the world they see in ways that change our vision of it. On this, the 100th Anniversary of the Corcoran School of Art, we salute our faculty, alumni and students for their work, their success and for sharing with us that vision. To find out about our Centennial Celebration, call 202-628-9484

The Corcoran School Of Art
for 100 years, Washington's Monument to Art

ICEBOX *Custom Framing*

Picture Framing Studio And Gallery, 2401 Central Avenue, Northeast Minneapolis, 612-788-1790

Art Director
Steven Mitsch
Copywriter

EEN GLAS HEERLIJKE VERSE MELK VERKWIKT EN GEEFT JE DIRECT WEER ENERGIE

MELK. DE WITTE MOTOR.

EEN GLAS HEERLIJKE VERSE MELK VERKWIKT EN GEEFT JE DIRECT WEER ENERGIE

MELK. DE WITTE MOTOR.

Client
van Ginneken & Mostaard
Art Director
Jan Pastoor
Copywriter
Kees Sterrenburg
Photographer
Ruud Posthuma
Illustrator
Raymond Lobato (Mieren)
Agency
PMSVW / Y & R

Client
Netherlands Zuivelbureau
Art Director
Pieter van Velsen
Copywriter
Aad Kuyper
Photographer
Will van der Vlugt
Agency
PPGH / JWT

Client
Jaguar Netherlands
Art Director
Clement Burger
Copywriter
Jan de Roos
Photographer
Chris Lewis
Agency
Kasperskoetse Burger and de Roos

DE NATTE DROOM

DE TOEKOMSTDROOM

Client
ETS
Art Director
Krijn van Noordwijk
Copywriter
Joeri Bakker
Photographer
Boudewijn Smit
Agency
Kuiper & Schouten

AUTO-EROTICISM.

HI. MY NAME'S JACK. I'M HERE TO SEE YOUR DAUGHTER.

He's an actor's actor and a studio executive's entry to paradise. He's also a rake, a charmer, a genius and a rogue. All these terms apply. To a reporter for LIFE, he sums it up with the internationally patented grin: "How I do love to play!"

LIFE was granted intimate access to Jack and his latest creations: Two Jakes and one baby, the latter an unexpected daughter with an actress in the film.

In the current tidal wave of Nicholson coverage, why does the most powerful actor in Hollywood feel comfortable offering LIFE his revelations? Maybe he sees his work as substantive and enduring, and thinks of LIFE the same way.

Client
LIFE Magazine
Designer
Ed Evangelista / Paul Wolfe
Photographer of Jack Nicholsen
Harry Benson

Client
LIFE Magazine
Designer
Ed Evangelista / Paul Wolfe
Photographer
Theo Westenberger

It's been a bumpy road for love these past decades.

In the 60's, you had free love. In the 70's, quick love. In the 80's, I'm-in-a-meeting-could-I-get-back-to-you love.

And now the indicators are in for the 90's. The winner? Yes, good old fashioned, committed, monogamous love.

Read it and sigh in LIFE's special Romance section. A comprehensive report on the state of the heart.

Photo: Mary Kelley

COMMITMENT IS BACK.

Client
LIFE Magazine
Designer
Ed Evangelista / Paul Wolfe
Photographer
Mary Kelley

A FACE ONLY FOUR PRESIDENTS COULD LOVE.

THERE ARE A LOT OF HORROR STORIES ABOUT SMALL TOWN GIRLS IN NEW YORK. THIS ISN'T ONE OF THEM.

FORMER KING LOOKING FOR WORK. WILLING TO RELOCATE.

VISIT YOUR GREAT GRANDPARENTS IN NEW YORK.

AMERICA. FROM SADDAM HUSSEIN'S POINT OF VIEW.

"DROP THE ELEPHANTS AND COME OUT WITH YOUR HANDS UP"

More dramatic Evangelista / Wolfe Ads
Photos
Manuel Noriega (Wesley Boxe / SIPA Press)
New York City street scene (Adler Gottfried)
Ellis Island Portraits (Watchorn Memorial
Methodist Church / Courtesy Metaform Inc.)
Elephants (Walter Unger)
Gulf War portraits (Harry Benson)
Former King (Jerard Rincinan)

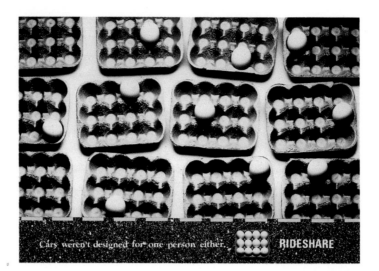

Cars weren't designed for one person either. RIDESHARE

Student work: J. Todd, W. Best

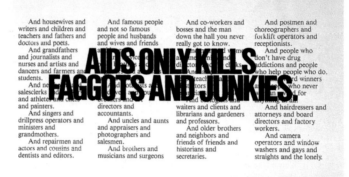

And housewives and writers and children and teachers and fathers and doctors and poets.
And grandfathers and journalists and nurses and artists and dancers and farmers and students.
And ne salesclerks and athlete and painters.
And singers and drillpress operators and ministers and grandmothers.
And repairmen and actors and cousins and dentists and editors.

And famous people and not so famous people and husbands and wives and friends

directors and accountants.
And uncles and aunts and appraisers and photographers and salesmen.
And brothers and musicians and surgeons

And co-workers and bosses and the man down the hall you never really got to know.

waiters and clients and librarians and gardeners and professors.
And older brothers and neighbors and friends of friends and historians and secretaries.

And postmen and choreographers and forklift operators and receptionists.
And people who don't have drug addictions and people who help people who do.
d winners who never for

And hairdressers and attorneys and board directors and factory workers.
And camera operators and window washers and gays and straights and the lonely.

AIDS ONLY KILLS FAGGOTS AND JUNKIES.

Get the facts. Call the AIDS Hotline: 800-922-2487

unidentified student

Chris Kosman

56

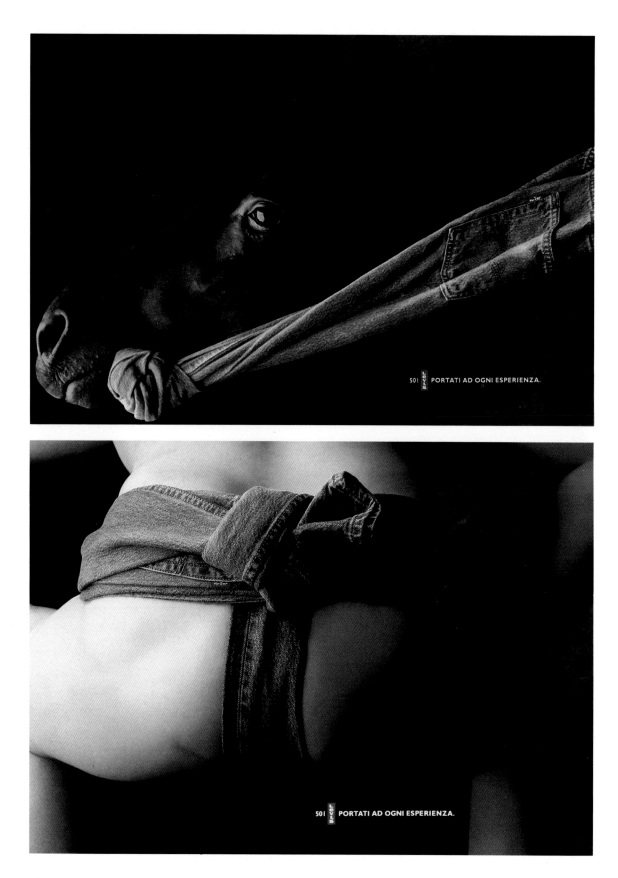

Client
Levi Strauss Italia

Art Director
Stefan Colombo

Creative Director
Milka Pogliani

Copywriter
Alessandro Canale

Photographer
Graham Ford

Agency
McCann - Erickson Italy

Client
Everlast
Art Director / Creative Director
Gary Goldsmith
Copywriter
Ty Montague
Agency
Goldsmith / Jeffrey

Client
The Dunham Company
Art Director / Creative Director
John Doyle
Copywriter
Ernie Schenck
Photographer
Nadav Kander
Agency
Doyle

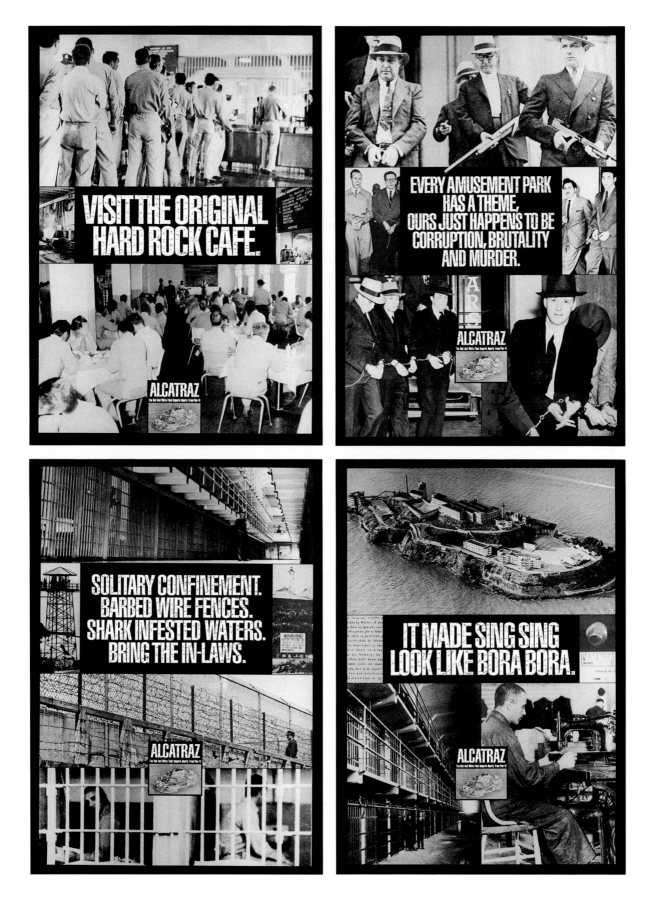

Client
The Red And White Fleet
Art Director
Michael Wilde
Creative Directors
Brian O´Neill
Mike Moser
Copywriter
Jim Noble
Agency
Goldberg Moser O´Neill

Client
Nynex Information
Resources
Art Director
Cabell Harris
Creative Director
Jay Chiat
Copywriter
Dion Hughes
Producer
Peter Franke
Photographer
Rick Dublin
Agency
Chiat / Day / Mojo

▶ **Bulldozing**

If it's out there, it's in here. **NYNEX Yellow Pages**

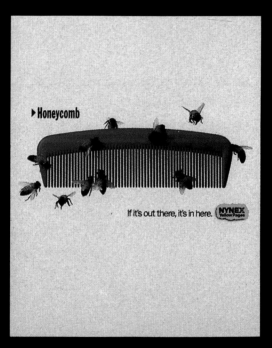

▶ Honeycomb

If it's out there, it's in here. **NYNEX Yellow Pages**

▶ **Letterheads**

If it's out there, it's in here. **NYNEX Yellow Pages**

Old cars go to scrap yards.
Old Porsches go to museums.

OUR FIRST PORSCHE: 1948 TYPE 356 ROADSTER.

PORSCHE

You may not have one
in your garage, but
you probably have one
parked in your mind.

PORSCHE

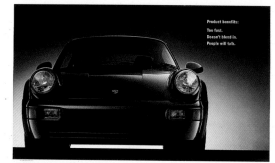

Product benefits:

Too fast.
Doesn't blend in.
People will talk.

PORSCHE

Client
Porsche Cars A. G.
Art Director
Tom Lichtenheld
Creative Director
Pat Burnham
Copywriter
Bruce Bildsten
Photographers
Andreas Burz
Lester Bookbinder
Daniel Jouanneau
Shawn Michienzi
Agency
Fallon McElligott

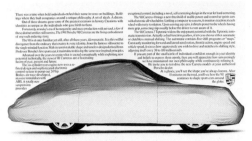

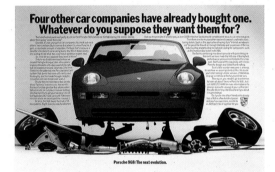

Client
Porsche Cars
North America
Art Director
Mark Johnson
Creative Director
Pat Burnham
Copywriter
John Stingley

Photographers
Jeff Zwart
Andreas Burz
Shawn Michienzi
Agency
Fallon McElligott

SO, YOU'RE FEELING A BIT GLOOMY THIS MORNING? READ ON. BY LUNCHTIME YOU CAN BE SUICIDAL.

1. Concentrate. How miserable *are* you exactly? A little 'down'? Depressed? Or on the verge of crying, stamping, and generally behaving like John McEnroe on one of his better days?

Is there a glimmer of hope on your personal horizon? Count your blessings. After all, the Straits Times has arrived without any evident signs of charring, so you can assume that the country's still in good hands. And, judging by the low growl not unadjacent to your left ear, you're still married.

Feeling worse, yet? Fine. Now we're getting somewhere.

2. Have you noticed that the lounges aren't open yet? This is obviously an oversight. Have these people no idea of how much hooch they could sell to those of us with a teeny-weeny little headache of a morning?

3. Outside the sun is shining.

4. This is no cause for merriment and joy. Sooner or later, you have to go out in it, and there's no brand of shades known to science or Michael Jackson that can protect a retina used only to the delicate pastels of neon, and the soothing glow of disco-strobes. This sunlight business is a killer.

5. Have you ever considered, in the light (is it too early for bad puns? It's always too early... OK) of the above, that you may be a vampire? Look in the mirror; are you there? Are you sure? If not, send out for a mallet, a stake, and someone who doesn't like you very much. Then brace yourself.

On the other hand, which blood-group do you prefer? It has to be cheaper than drinking Beck's, which is some consolation, I guess.

6. Beck's Beer is outrageously, unfairly, expensive. Ordinary beer isn't.

7. Life itself is unfair. (See above).

8. It is, you'll agree, the rich what gets the pleasure, and the poor what gets the blame. The poor also gets the sticky end of every other deal going: Viz and to whit, no Beck's. If you are poor, you'll agree that this, too, is very unfair indeed. If you are rich, get on with your Beck's. And I hope you drown in it.

9. One red traffic-light is always followed by another red traffic-light.

10. Especially when you're in a hurry.

11. More especially when you're late for an appointment you wish you hadn't made in the first place.

12. And when you get there, wringing wet, with anxiety and exertion, your appointment is always later still.

13. When he arrives, he is always calm, composed, and dry as a pawnbroker's eye.

14. You are not allowed to kill him. It is apparently frowned upon in polite circles. Unwarranted pickiness, in our view.

15. When you're young, fit, and attractive, you haven't got any money, so the girls ignore you.

16. When you get older, and richer, you also get fat, ugly, and bald. The girls suddenly show a bizarre preference for younger, poorer men.

17. If you have a full head of hair, girls tell you that bald men are sexy.

18. If you are bald, this previously immutable fact seems to escape them.

19. Life's a bitch. Then you marry one.

20. On the other hand, there's always Bangkok. Or Manila.

21. Or Aids.

22. Becks is a lot more expensive than ordinary beers. Have we mentioned the fact before? It's preying on our minds. With some justification.

23. Buttered toast, when dropped, always lands butter-side down. This well-known law of physics could be the answer to life, the Universe, and everything. The answer previously having been believed to be 48.

24. Lawyers are allowed to wear curly wigs, and long black frocks.

25. Gentlemen who are *not* lawyers, but wear long black frocks and curly wigs, are likely to be sent to jail. By lawyers wearing long black frocks and curly wigs. Or, if they're top-gun type lawmen, in *long* curly wigs, and long *red* frocks. (Black stockings, suspenders, and frilly underwear are apparently purely optional, in either case).

26. Lawyers are allowed to drink Beck's and they can afford it, too. This is very, very irritating indeed.

27. Ben Hunt cannot afford Beck's but still drinks it. Mind you, he'll drink *anything*.

28. The bad guys frequently win.

29. Unless you happen to *be* a bad guy, in which case, welcome to Changi; this is your bucket. Enjoy.

30. The makers and sellers of Beck's are allowed to roam the streets, despite the fact that they are horrid, larcenous, greedy, and totally devoid of humanity.

31. A man who trifles with the affections of defenceless young girls should be damn well hung. And usually, is.

32. It is impossible to get a decent hot pastrami sandwich in Singapore. This is especially peeving when you consider how well hot pastrami-on-rye goes down with a nice, cold, Beck's.

33. On the other hand, nearly anything goes down nicely with Beck's, except the price of the Beck's, which gives you raging indigestion. If this is fair, then I'm a Chinaman. Which I'm not, so that proves it.

34. You may well *be* a Chinaman, and if you can afford Beck's, I hate you, and in any case, it's your round.

35. When you get home, late and drunk, the wife is always wide-awake, waiting.

36. When you get home early and sober, she's gone to her Mother's for the night. This is occasionally referred-to as Sod's Law. As opposed to Murphy's. (see 23).

37. That delightful seventeen-year-old over there is going to look like her Mother one day.

38. Unless her Mother's beautiful, in which case she'll grow to look like her Dad. Or, alternatively, her goldfish.

39. If you lived in Europe, you could buy a Mercedes for the same price as a mid-range Japanese car costs here. A Rolls-Royce, here, costs the same as a three-bedroom apartment in London. Wherever you live, Beck's is ridiculously expensive, so you may as well stay home.

40. No matter how much money you earn, you spend it.

41. Copywriters get paid absurd amounts of money for writing reams of stuff that nobody bothers to read. This, for instance. They then spend most of it on loose women, fast cars, and Beck's, and just waste the rest. This is absolutely, incredibly unfair, and I don't give a hoot.

Nobody in their right mind would pay this kind of money for a beer. Now, if someone could just help me out of this strait-jacket...

42. Is it lunchtime yet? Oddly enough I feel *much* better now. Think I'll go and have a Becks.

43. Hang the expense.

Designer
Neil French
Photographer
Alex Kaikeong

Designer
Neil French

Designer
Neil French
Photographer
Alex Kaikeong

IF A DUTCHMAN CAN GET THE JAPANESE TO PAY EIGHTY MILLION BUCKS FOR A VASE OF FLOWERS, MAYBE YOU SHOULD LET ONE HANDLE YOUR CASH.

The Dutch have been smart businessmen for centuries. Juggling currencies, commodities, and shares, to end up with a profit is second nature to them. You might say it's an art form.

So it could well be worth your while talking to us at ABN Bank (the largest international Dutch bank) about our Discretionary Currency Management service.

In simple terms, this means that we shift cash from currency to currency, according to the exchange rates, and use our considerable experience with the aim of ending up with a profit for our clients.

If you'd like the full picture, call us and ask for details. After all, although we're bankers, we're Dutch, so we'll be happy to lend you our ears. **ABN Bank**

THE DUTCH ARE FAMOUS FOR GROWING THINGS.

LIKE TULIPS. AND RICH.

One of the very best times to visit Holland is in the Spring, when the flowers are beginning to bloom.

Visitors from all over the world pour into the country to marvel at the oceans of colour. There's nothing quite like it, anywhere.

In fact, tourists are often amazed to see the normally rather phlegmatic and practical Dutch, themselves gazing at the view with undisguised emotion.

After all, a tear in a Dutchman's eye is often thought to be as rare as a diamond.

At the risk of destroying illusion, we should perhaps point out that this emotional local, while hardly immune to the beauties of nature, is more likely to have been overcome by the thought of all the money he's making.

The massive profits from flower exports!

The huge income from tourism, as folks fly in specially to gaze in wonder at fields of living cash!

This, of course, does not make the Dutch soulless, merely, as we've said before, practical.

(In any case, a nation dedicated to making money from flowers, beer, and gin can only be seen as having a delightful sense of proportion!)

What it does indicate is that if you're looking for someone to manage your money you'd do well to consult a Dutchman.

To be precise: us.

ABN Bank is Holland's largest international bank, and we've been here in Singapore for well over a hundred years, quietly and efficiently making Singaporeans richer.

For the private investor, we can offer two particularly interesting schemes.

One is the discretionary or non-discretionary Investment Account; the other is the very topical discretionary Currency Management scheme.

This means we juggle currencies with the aim of making you money. It's a knack we have.

Why not give us a call?

We're easy to get on with and, together, we might grow you a fortune. **ABN Bank**

Client
ABN / Amro Bank
Designer
Neil French

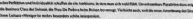

Client
Swissair Deutschland
Art Director
Lucia Frey
Creative Director
Ernst Baechtold
Copywriter
Nhur Barguil
Photographer
Alberto Venzago
Agency
GGK Zürich
Werbeagentur AG

Client
Bernd Berger Mode GmbH
Art Director
Carlos Ferreira
Creative Director / Photographer
Heinrich Hoffmann
Agency
Heinrich Hoffmann & Partner

3x Vietnam
1x Kambodscha
2x Nordirland
1x Libanon
1x Äthiopien
2x Sri Lanka
1x Nicaragua
1x China
4x Rumänien

1x in Reparatur.

Außen Giugiaro.

Groß, schwer, kompliziert und teuer.

Innen Nikon.

Client
Nikon GmbH
Copywriter
Stefan Teleqdy
Creative Director
Jürgen Werth
Photographers
Axel Gnad
Ivo v. Renner

Diese Herren schießen die meisten Tore der Bundesliga.

Sie kommen fast nie zum Training, stehen bei jeder Begegnung am Spielfeldrand und haben trotzdem eine Trefferquote, die jeder Mannschaft den Pokal sichern würde: die Sportfotografen. Wer bei diesem Verein mitspielen möchte, muß schon einiges bringen. Denn ein gutes Auge, schnelles Reaktionsvermögen und eine sichere Hand gehören genauso dazu wie die richtige Kamera. Ist es unsportlich zu sagen, daß die meisten Profis sich da ganz auf uns eingespielt haben?

Nikon
Das Auge der Welt.

Eine Nikon muß jahrelanges Schütteln ohne Ausfälle überstehen.

Unsere Profikamera F4 kann so gut wie nichts mehr erschüttern. Denn sie muß bereits während der Produktion Hunderte von Kontrollen und Tests über sich ergehen lassen. Und die aufwendige Technik und die robuste Mechanik geben einem weitaus mehr als nur das Gefühl von Sicherheit.

Wenn sich in Bonn zwei Menschen länger als 45 Sekunden die Hand geben, ist das meist so wichtig, daß wir das Bild am nächsten Tag in der Zeitung sehen. Und deshalb wimmelt es nur so von Bildberichterstattern, wenn der Kanzler mal Besuchszeit hat. Jeder von ihnen weiß, daß bereits die ersten Aufnahmen sitzen müssen, weil Politikern das Lächeln oft schnell vergeht. Das könnte auch der Grund sein, warum so viele unserer Kameras in die Politik gehen.

Nikon
Das Auge der Welt.

Client
Borco Markenimport, HH
Art Director
Ulla Nagelschmitz
Creative Directors
Gerald Heinemann
Ewald Wolf
Olaf Oldigs
Copywriters
Olaf Oldigs
Carsten Blatt
Photographer
Siggi Kercher
Agency
Scholz & Friends GmbH

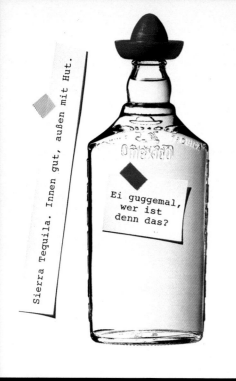

Client	*Copywriters*
Weltmarken Imp.	Carlos Obers, Gudrun Müllner,
Art Director	Jörg Jahn, Barbara Stuck
Gudrun Müllner	*Illustrator*
Creative Director	Gudrun Müllner
Carlos Obers	*Agency*
Designer	RG Wiesmeier Werbeagentur

Client
Crisan Wella AG
Art Director
Silke Niehaus
Creative Director
Gerd Simon
Copywriter
Michael Bonzio
Agency
Hildmann, Simon, Rempen & Schmitz / SMS

Client
R. J. Reynolds Tobacco
Art Directors
Harald Schmidt
Bettina Holzinger
Andrea Schmidt
Creative Directors
Michael Preiswerk
Uwe Vock
Designers
Ina Mielkau
Thomas Gessner
Copywriters
Sven Stephan
Oliver Hesse
Katherine Schwartz
Agency
McCann - Erickson Frankfort

LORENZINI

Client
Lorenzini
Art Director
Terry Jones
Photographer
Robert Erdmann

Unpublished Clearasil ad by
Jean-Paul Goude

Photo '93 is a compilation of over 300 images selected from a worldwide call for entries. □ **Graphis Typography 1** spans the years from the "founding fathers" of type design through the modern masters. A comprehensive time line, examples of computer aided type design and pictorial displays of past and present designers make this book invaluable. □ **Design '94** a classic Graphis annual with 700 examples of visual communication spanning 256 pages with such categories as design, illustration, advertising, brochures, letterheads and more. □ **Poster '93** contains over 400 images and 256 pages and features introductions by Ron Dumas: Creative Director/Graphic Designer of Nike footwear, Makoto Saito, Japanese poster illustrator and Catherine Bürer of the Swiss Poster Collection. □ **Graphis Nudes** with 224 pages and over 200 images, this book is an elegant and impressive collection of carefully

selected images by the world's outstanding photographers. □ **Graphis Annual Reports 4** features the best in annual report design from fiscal 1991 and 1992. These reports are selected based, not only on outstanding design style, but also for excellence in photography, illustration and over-all composition. □ **Letterhead 2** is suited to guide and inspire the graphic designer in creating strong visual identities. □ **Graphis Paper Specifier System (GPS)** includes cross referenced indexes organized by paper manufacturer and paper name, region of merchant directory and factual paper information. □ **Logo 2** extensive in scope, the book is packed with over 300 innovative top-quality logos, created for both large and small firms, as well as not-for-profit foundations and organizations. □ **Photo '93** ist eine Sammlung von über 300 Bildern, die auf Grund ihrer künstlerischen Qualität

anlässlich des neusten internationalen Graphis-Wettbewerbs ausgewählt wurden. □ **Graphis Typography 1** bietet ein breites Panorama der Schriftgestaltung, von den Anfängen der Typographie bis hin zu Schriften, die mit dem Computer entwickelt wurden. Eine zeitliche Übersicht führt von den «Gründervätern» zu den modernen Meistern, dokumentiert durch zahlreiche Abbildungen. □ **Design '94**, der Klassiker der Graphis-Jahrbücher, zeigt weit mehr als 700 Beispiele visueller Kommunikation (Gestaltung von Broschüren, Anzeigen, Zeitschriften, Briefköpfen etc.). 256 Seiten Design total. □ **Poster '93** enthält über 400 Bilder. Eingeleitet wird der 256 Seiten starke Band mit Texten von Ron Dumas, Creative Director/Graphic Designer für Nike-Schuhe, von Makoto Saito, dem japanischen Plakatkünstler, und von Catherine Bürer, Direktorin der

Plakatsammlung des Museums für Gestaltung, Zürich. □ **Graphis Nudes** versammelt auf 224 Seiten 200 sorgfältig ausgewählte Aktphotos von hervorragenden Photographen aus aller Welt. □ **Graphis Annual Reports 4** zeigt Jahresberichte für 1991 und 1992. Beurteilt wurde die Gestaltung, aber auch die Qualität von Illustrationen und Photographie sowie der Produktion. □ **Letterhead 2** bietet Anregung und Inspiration bei der Gestaltung ausserordentlicher visueller Erscheinungsbilder. □ **Graphis Paper Specifier System (GPS)** enthält Papiermuster sowie Indexe nach Herstellern und Papiersorten, Händlerverzeichnisse und Angaben zu den Papieren. □ **Logo 2** zeigt ein breites Spektrum von 300 innovativen, hervorragenden Logos für kleine und grosse Betriebe, Institutionen und Organisationen. □ **Photo '93** est un recueil

de plus de 300 illustrations choisies pour leur qualité artistique à l'occasion d'un concours international. □ **Graphis Typography 1** présente un panorama exhaustif du design typographique, des pionniers de l'ancienne génération aux plus grands créateurs actuels. Vous y trouverez aussi bien des exemples de typographies élaborées sur ordinateur que des créations de designers d'hier et d'aujourd'hui. □ **Design '94** présente plus de 700 exemples de communication visuelle (création de brochures, d'annonces, de publications, de papiers à entête etc.). □ **Poster '93** contient plus de 400 images. La préface de cet ouvrage de 256 pages est signée par Ron Dumas, directeur artistique et graphiste de la marque de chaussures Nike, Makoto Saito, le créateur d'affiches japonais, et par Catherine Bürer, conservatrice de la collection d'affiche du Museum für Gestaltung à Zurich. □ **Graphis**

Nudes rassemble sur 224 pages 200 des plus belles photos des grands photographes contemporains. □ **Graphis Annual Reports 4** présente le meilleur des rapports annuels de 1991 et 1992. Les rapports sont choisies essentiellement en fonction de leur composition, mais aussi pour leur valeur sur le plan de photo ou du dessin et leur qualité de production. □ **Letterhead 2** offre aux graphistes une source d'inspiration pour la création de fortes identités visuelles. □ **Graphis Paper Specifier System (GPS)** contient des échantillons de papier ainsi qu'un index des fabricants et des différentes variétés de papier, un annuaire des représentants ainsi que diverses informations. □ **Logo 2** présente un vaste éventail de 300 logos pleins d'innovation et de très haute qualité conçus pour les entreprises de toutes tailles ainsi que pour les organisations à but non-lucratif. □